THE DOG GOSPELS

THE DOG GOSPELS

Inspirations from Our Best Friends

WILLOW CREEK PRESS
Minocqua, Wisconsin

© 2002 Willow Creek Press

Published by Willow Creek Press
P.O. Box 147
Minocqua, Wisconsin 54548

All rights reserved. No part of this book may
be reproduced or transmitted in any form by
any means, electronic or mechanical, includ-
ing photocopying, recording, or by any information storage and retrieval system, without
written permission from the Publisher.

For information on other Willow Creek
titles, call 1-800-850-9453

**Library of Congress
Cataloging-in-Publication Data**
The dog gospels : spiritual inspirations from
our best friends.
    p. cm.
    ISBN 1-57223-589-6 (alk. paper)
    1. Dogs--Religious aspects. 2. Spiritual
life. I. Willow Creek Press.
    BL443.D64 D64 2002
    291.4'32--dc21
                            2002010157

Printed in Canada

PHOTOGRAPHER CREDITS

Listed by page number: 2 ©Kent & Donna Dannen;
6, 7 ©Denver Bryan; 08 ©Ron Kimball; 10 ©Cheryl A.
Ertelt; 11 ©Terry Wild Studio; 12 ©Denver Bryan;
14 ©Bonnie Nance; 16 ©Jean M. Fogle; 17 ©Robert
Kaufman/Silver Visions; 18 ©Ron Kimball; 21 ©Karen
Hudson; 22 ©Sharon Eide & Elizabeth Flynn;
24 ©Bonnie Nance; 25 ©Chris Luneski/Image Cascade;
26 ©Pitlik Studio; 28 ©Cheryl A. Ertelt; 29 ©Ed
Camelli; 30 ©Nancy McCallum; 31 ©Bonnie Nance;
32 ©Tara Darling; 33 ©Terry Wild Studio;
34 ©Bonnie Nance; 35, 37 ©Denver Bryan;
38 ©Bonnie Nance; 40 ©Robert Kaufman/Silver
Visions; 42 ©Bonnie Nance; 43 ©Daniel Dempster;
44 ©Terry Wild Studio; 46 ©Ed Simpson; 47 ©Terry
Wild Studio; 48 ©Denver Bryan; 50 ©Ron Kimball;
51 ©Terry Wild Studio; 52 ©Bonnie Nance; 53 ©Chris
Luneski/Image Cascade; 54 ©Cris Kelly; 55 ©Larry &
Marge Grant; 56 ©Bonnie Nance; 58 ©Ron Kimball;
58 ©Terry Wild Studio; 60 ©Ron Kimball; 61 ©Norvia
Behling; 62 ©Terry Wild Studio; 63 ©Ron Kimball;
64 ©Terry Wild Studio; 66 ©Terry Wild Studio;
67 ©Bonnie Nance; 68 ©Cheryl A. Ertelt; 70 ©MM
David Lorenz Winston; 71 ©Daniel Dempster;
72 ©Sharon Eide & Elizabeth Flynn; 74 ©Denver
Bryan; 75 ©Ron Kimball; 76 ©Terry Wild Studio;
77 ©Bonnie Nance; 78 ©Kent & Donna Dannen;
80 ©Louisa Preston; 81 ©Kent & Donna Dannen;
82 ©Denver Bryan; 84 ©Pets by Paulette; 85 ©Bonnie
Nance; 86 ©Nancy McCallum; 88 ©Sharon Eide &
Elizabeth Flynn; 89 ©Ron Kimball; 90 ©Ron Kimball;
92 ©Bonnie Nance; 93 ©Terry Wild Studio;
94 ©Daniel Dempster; 96 ©Terry Wild Studio.

With apologies to all persons living or dead
whose words have been twisted by these dogs.

THE EDITORS

℥hose who help others are helped.

THE SERVICE DOG'S CREED

$\mathcal{A}$ cheerful disposition is good
for your health.
Gloom and doom
Leave you bone-tired.
<small>THE BOOK OF BEN</small>

God respects me when I
work but he loves me when I sing.

PLACIDO DOGINGO

Whether one believes in a religion or not . . . there isn't anyone who doesn't appreciate kindness and compassion.

MUTTHATMA GHANDHI

Live the actual moment. Only this moment is life.

LABS II, 3:7

In the practice of tolerance, one's enemy is the best teacher.

LABBA RAM DAS

Please, Lord, make
me pure . . .
but not just yet.

ST. BERNARD

Outside ideas of right doing and wrong doing there is a field. I'll meet you there.

Rumi Rin Tin

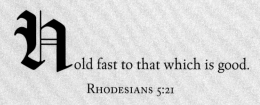

old fast to that which is good.

RHODESIANS 5:21

$\mathfrak{I}$f ye have faith, nothing shall be
impossible for you.

THE RETRIEVER'S CREED

Watch
therefore: for ye
know not what hour
your master
shall come.
THE WATCHDOG'S
MANUAL

Who out there has a lust for life? Can't wait each day to play and chase?

Labs I 3:9

$\mathcal{G}$reat things are done more through fear than wisdom.

BONE SOUP FOR THE SOUL

A good friend who points out mistakes and imperfections is to be respected as if she reveals the secret of some hidden bone.

LABBA RAM DAS

Seeking God is like finding a path in the snow.
If there is no path, begin to walk. Look back and
there is your path. Now continue to walk.

SIBERIAN HUSKY PROVERB

Woe to those who stint

the measure.

THE K-9 BIBLE

$\mathcal{A}$ righteous master cares
for the needs of his animals.
GOOD NEWS FOR MODERN DOGS

A faithful friend is a strong defense; and he that hath found such a friend has found a treasure.

THE BOOK OF THE DOG

May our perfect happiness
be found in heaven,
where dogs and humans shall
reside together in eternity.

A DOG'S PRAYER

There is no greater illusion than fear.

SHI TSU

The earth trembled and a great rift appeared, separating the first man and woman from the rest of the animal kingdom. As the chasm grew deeper and wider, all the other creatures, afraid for their lives, returned to the forest — except for the dog who, after much consideration, leapt the perilous rift to stay with the humans on the other side. His love for humanity [and their way of preparing succulent bison steaks] was greater than his bond to other creatures, he explained, and he willingly forfeited his place in paradise to prove it.

NATIVE FIDO FOLKTALE

So many dogs, so many breeds;
So many friends to meet and greet,
While caring and tolerance and kindness
Are all this sad world needs.

I Goldens 4:12-16

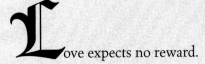

Love expects no reward.

Love knows no fear.

THE POWER OF PUPPYHOOD

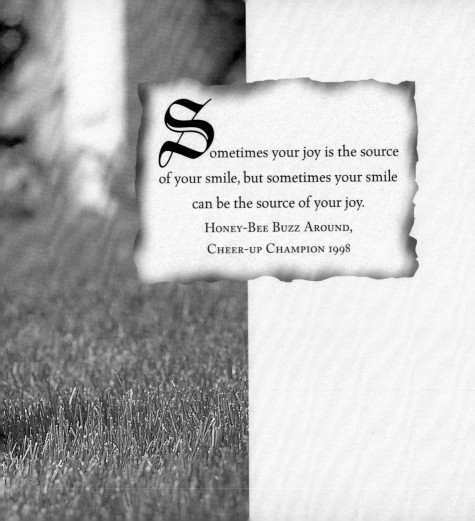

Sometimes your joy is the source of your smile, but sometimes your smile can be the source of your joy.

HONEY-BEE BUZZ AROUND,
CHEER-UP CHAMPION 1998

Because straight is the gate, and

narrow the way . . .

Few there be that find it.

I GOLDENS 5: 17

The Bird of Time
is on the wing
and has but little way to go,
so fill your cup to the brim
and let your love overflow.

Spot of Smith's Acres

Find joy in your work and not just your play;

for your work may at any time

become your play.

YUKON JACK, AUTHOR OF PULL TO WIN

Don't try to
lead me or to be
led by me; just
walk beside me
and be my friend.

II GOLDENS, 7: 14

51

Not only the thirsty seek water, the water as well seeks the thirsty.

RUMI RIN TIN

$\mathcal{A}$sk, and it shall
be given to you;
seek, and ye shall find;
knock and it shall be
opened unto you.

THE BOOK OF THE DOG

Do not keep the polished bones of your friendship
buried until your friends are dead. Fill their lives with sweetness.
Speak approving, cheering words while their ears can hear them,
and while their hearts can be thrilled and made happier.
The treats you mean to give when they are gone,
present to them before they go.

DOLLY LABBA

The Power of the World always works in circles, and everything tries to be round. The sky is round, and I have heard that the earth is round like a ball, and so are the stars. The wind, in its greatest power, whirls. Birds make their nests in circles, and we too must turn in circles before we can lie down.

LABBA RAM DAS

The grace of the master is like an ocean. If one comes with a cup he will get only a cupful. It is no use complaining. The bigger the vessel the more one will be able to carry. It's entirely up to him.

SPOT OF SMITH'S ACRES

Our sins are created in secrecy. The moment we realize that the human witnesses even our thoughts we shall be free.

THE POWER OF PUPPYHOOD

Dogma is like fashion: One dog wears his collar tagged, another studded, another plain, but every pup has a collar; so every dog has a dogma. We simply differ about the trimmings.

St. Bernard

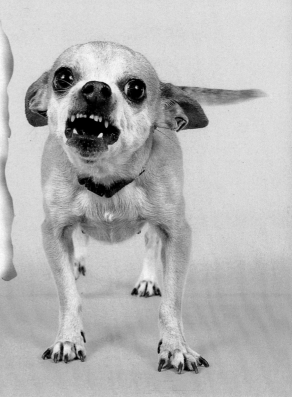

If you deny the existence of your fault or error, it will strengthen its hold over you.

RECOVERY STEP TWO,
BITERS ANONYMOUS

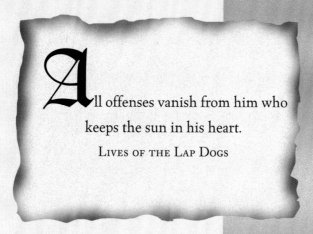

All offenses vanish from him who keeps the sun in his heart.

LIVES OF THE LAP DOGS

All animals, even those of the same species, are not alike, and it is the same with dogs. The reason the Creator does not make two dogs, or any two animals exactly alike is because each is placed here to be an independent individuality and to rely upon itself.

THE SIMPLE SHEPHERD

That which we call sin in others, is
experiment for us.

St. Bernard

Love is patient, love is kind. It does not envy, it does not boast, it is not proud. It is not rude, it is not easily angered, it keeps no record of wrongs. Love does not delight in evil but rejoices with truth. It always protects, always trusts, always perseveres. A dog is love.

THE GOSPEL ACCORDING TO SKIP

Live your life as a prayer.

DOLLY LABBA

Health is the greatest gift, contentment
the greatest wealth, the faithfulness of
a dog the best relationship.

ANONYMUTT

The plainest sign of wisdom
is a continual cheerfulness;
the way there is like the wake
of a duck on smooth water.

THE BOOK OF RACHEL 12:3-4

$\mathcal{A}$chieve greatness in little things; thus
the simple shall be complicated and the
complicated becomes simple.

THE WAY OF THE WEIMARANER

I celebrate myself, and sing myself.

QUEENIE WHITMAN,
AUTHOR OF LEAVES OF YELLOW GRASS

Neither time nor the faulty memory of humans, neither birth nor death can erase our good deeds.

THE SERVICE DOG'S CREED

Our plans miscarry if they have no aim. When a dog does not know what harbor he is making for, no wind is the right wind.

BITERS ANONYMOUS HANDBOOK

Life must be lived as play.

ROVER'S GUIDE TO THE UNIVERSE

My daily affairs are quite ordinary; but I'm in total harmony with them. I don't hold on to anything, don't reject anything; nowhere an obstacle or conflict. Who cares about wealth and honour? Even the poorest thing shines. My miraculous power and spiritual activity? Fetching and carrying sticks for those who ask.

LABBA RAM DAS

Suffer the unjust punishments of those less worthy, knowing that one day the door will be opened to you, and you will be free.

The Gospel according to Skip

We should conduct ourselves toward others as we would have them act toward us.

THE WAY OF THE
WEIMARANER

Be a bud sitting quietly on the hedge. Be a smell, one part of wondrous existence. Sit and stay. There is no need to depart.

DOLLY LABBA

Craziness is good. Crazy dogs are happy, free, they have no
inhibitions. You must become completely crazy.

Then you will understand.

THE LIVES OF THE LAP DOGS

Work as though you would live forever, and live as though you would die today.

THE BOOK OF THE DOG

Keep me away from the wisdom which does
not cry, the philosophy which does not laugh,
and the greatness which does not bow before children.

SPOT OF SMITH'S ACRES

"**I** have done my best." That is about all the philosophy of living a dog needs.

THE BOOK OF THE DOG

The path to God is whatever path you're on . . . just follow your nose.

ROVER'S GUIDE TO THE UNIVERSE